Otherwise Bob

CONNIE GAULT

Otherwise Bob
first published 1999 by
Scirocco Drama
An imprint of J. Gordon Shillingford Publishing Inc.
© 1996 Connie Gault

Scirocco Drama Series Editor: Dave Carley
Cover design by Terry Gallagher/Doowah Design Inc.
Author photo by Dylan Gault

Printed and bound in Canada

Published with the financial assistance of The Canada Council for the Arts
and the Manitoba Arts Council.

"Some Enchanted Evening" from *South Pacific*, by Rodgers and Hammerstein.
Rights held by Williamson Music, 1633 Broadway, Suite 3801, New York, NY 10019.

Canadian Cataloguing in Publication Data

Gault, Connie, 1949-
    Otherwise Bob

A play.
ISBN 1-896239-49-8
    I. Title.
PS8563.A8445O85 1999 C812'.54   C99-900152-3
PR9199.3.G374O85 1999

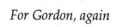

For Gordon, again

Connie Gault lives in Regina where she writes plays and fiction. Her most recent book is the short story collection, *Inspection of a Small Village* (Coteau, 1996). She has written three stage plays (*Otherwise Bob*, *The Soft Eclipse* and *Sky*) and several radio dramas. From 1995 to 1998, she was the fiction editor for *Grain* magazine. She has been an active and appreciative member of the Saskatchewan Play-wrights Centre for longer than she can remember.

Production History

Otherwise Bob received simultaneous premieres by Northern Light Theatre and by Alberta Theatre Projects (as part of playRites '96) in January, 1996 with the following casts:

MARIE/ANNE .... Patricia Casey
ALBERT/JOHN/WAITER .... Richard Gishler
BOB .... Brian Linds
DAVID .... Michael Spencer-Davis
JENNIFER .... Marina Stephenson Kerr
GIRL .... Caitlin Varrin
VOICES .... Cara Alexander, Helen Anne Fulford,
Rebecca Murtha, Kate O'Gorman

Directed by D.D. Kugler
Set and Costume Design by Dave Boechler
Composition/Sound Design by Binaifer Kapadia
Lighting Design by Melinda Sutton
Production Coordinator: Jim Bob Boudreau
Stage Manager: Marian Brant
Production Manager: Cheryl Hood

JENNIFER .... Kate Newby
BOB .... Tom Rooney
ALBERT/JOHN/WAITER .... Paul Punyi
ANNE/MARIE .... Maureen Thomas
GIRL .... Brittany Lyons
DAVID .... Daryl Shuttleworth

Directed by Patti Shedden
Set Design by Terry Gunvordahl
Costume Design by Judith Bowden
Lighting Design by Brian Pincott
Composer: Richard McDowell
Production Dramaturge: Bob White
Assistant Designer: Leslie Bush

Acknowledgements

I received a Canada Council grant to write this play and I am deeply grateful for the financial assistance and the trust that support implies. During the writing of many drafts of a script that seemed to have a will and a logic of its own, I was sustained by my family whose patience was phenomenal—Gord, Dylan, Brennan, once again, thank you—and by my friends, Marlis Wesseler and Dianne Warren, whose patience finally and luckily wore out, forcing me to finish the play. As usual, I want to thank Marina Endicott, too, for our long conversations about theatre. Particular thanks to Patti Shedden, who was the first reader of the play and who responded with such generosity. Then I want to thank Candace Burley and Iris Turcott for the Canadian Stage Company reading, the Saskatchewan Playwright Centre and Bob White for a wonderful partly staged reading, D.D. Kugler for his meticulous dramaturgy, Northern Light Theatre and Alberta Theatre Projects for two very different simultaneous first productions, and Ruth Smillie and Globe Theatre for bringing the play home to Regina. There are many others— theatre professionals and audience members—whose comments helped me shape this script. For her insights and support, I especially thank Joanne Lyons.

Characters

JENNIFER
BOB
ALBERT/JOHN/WAITER
MARIE/ANNE
DAVID
GIRL

Notes on the Characters

BOB, ALBERT, and sometimes JENNIFER are often pleased with their physical and verbal choices and indicate that pleasure.

BOB is a liminal character. He is meant to be somewhat insubstantial. His body follows wherever his hand leads.

ALBERT is tentative. He keeps his balls (small beach balls, about the size of balloons) in a sports bag that is often unzipped.

MARIE is frightening to see. Her catatonia is abstract, almost elemental. Occasionally, without drawing attention to herself, she changes position. Her poses make her look like Henry Moore sculptures. Her face reveals her determination to block out everything, to think no thoughts.

DAVID is a kind person who is frustrated in all his attempts to control his life.

JOHN and ANNE are older friends of the couple. They are afraid of silence and of the kind of language that allows silence, with good reason.

The GIRL is about 11 years old.

The doubling of ALBERT/JOHN/WAITER and MARIE/ANNE is intentional and for artistic (not economic) reasons.

Notes on the Text

Dialogue is often broken into paragraphs to indicate the character is expecting some response from another, or listening to a silent self-response before proceeding. This creates half-pauses or quarter-pauses. Throughout the dialogue, pauses should be found to accentuate the dream-like nature of the play and silences should be employed to create dream-like (as opposed to movie-like) suspense.

Dashes after a speech indicate an interruption, either external or internal.

Dashes before a speech indicate a character is interrupting another.

Notes for Production

The play is a manifestation of JENNIFER's mind. The production should help the audience share her point of view.

The selections of music noted in the stage directions are not necessarily the only choices, but they are given because they are the music I heard while writing.

Ideally, the play is produced without an intermission.

Part One

(BOB's house and bookstore.

JENNIFER stands alone; she may be in the Henry Moore room at the Ontario Art Gallery or on a street in her city or in her own backyard. There are still shapes around her: sculptures or shadows or trees. Something makes her think of her mother. She may see BOB pass by in the distance. A wedge-shaped shadow falls over her. She looks toward what will be the bookstore.

ALBERT appears in the bookstore, sitting with his bag open on his lap. He is bobbing his head into the balls that fill the bag, feeling his song building in him.

BOB enters to the sudden loud music of the opening to Tchaikovsky's "Piano Concerto No. 1". BOB's right hand sways to the music. He follows his hand joyously, though not without difficulty, up and down the aisles.)

ALBERT: "Some enchanted evening—
Some enchanted evening—

(A door opens, letting a triangle of light fall into BOB's path. BOB uses his left hand to steer his right so that his body follows his right hand out of the way of the opening door.)

Some enchanted evening—"

(JENNIFER enters the bookstore and stands for several seconds with the sunlight falling on her. She has a fish wrapped in brown paper in her hands and she twists it as she talks.)

JENNIFER: Excuse me—?

(BOB has difficulty directing himself to a position in which he can speak to her. As the music fades, he slows. JENNIFER has difficulty making contact to speak to him.)

Hi—

Hi. I'm looking for a book.

It's about a girl who grows up in the Everglades or some exotic place.

There are trees—

The girl collects moths—

Or maybe butterflies— and her mother is mean to her.

BOB: That would be *A Girl of the Limberlost*.

JENNIFER: Yes. That's right. I loved it. When I was a girl.

BOB: Unfortunately I haven't got a copy.

And I'm afraid it's out of print so you'll have some difficulty finding it.

ALBERT: "Some enchanted evening—"

BOB: I could make a note of your name. If we get one second-hand, I could call you.

JENNIFER: I wanted it today.

BOB: Yes, I understand.

(JENNIFER begins to cry, surprising herself.)

Have you tried the library?

JENNIFER: I'm sorry. It's silly to cry over a book.

BOB: Would you leave your name? Let me get a pen.

JENNIFER: I'm sorry. This is silly. I'm standing here crying.

BOB: Let me take your name.

JENNIFER: That's okay. Really.

(ALBERT hands BOB a note. BOB passes it to JENNIFER.)

(Reads.) "Caregiver required. To look after a woman who can't look after herself. This is a live-in position, with a one-room suite provided. Apply here."

But—I don't want a job.

I don't need a job. I couldn't look after someone else. I have a job, a home and a husband. If I were someone else—

But I'm not. I couldn't walk out of one life into another. Just like that.

ALBERT: She could try it.

JENNIFER: What?

BOB: You could try it.

JENNIFER: I'd have to be a different person.

People don't...

I'd have to see the woman. I'd have to see the house.

ALBERT: She could knock on that door.

Why, it's no more to knock on that door than to open one of these books and read.

JENNIFER: It would be simple, if you didn't think too much about it.

             (*JENNIFER shudders.*

             Now, it seems a door has opened by itself and BOB is on the other side.)

             I've come regarding the job. The job of looking after the woman who can't look after herself?

BOB: You've come to apply?

JENNIFER: I've come to see the woman and the house.

BOB: You understand it's a live-in job? We offer a one-room suite. I can show you that. Through this hall.

JENNIFER: It's very dark and narrow. Very dark and narrow.

BOB: That would be your door, at the end of the hall. Should you decide to accept the job.

JENNIFER: Whose door would this be?

BOB: That's my father's door.

JENNIFER: And your mother?

BOB: She lives upstairs.

JENNIFER: Is she the woman who can't look after herself?

BOB: Yes she is.

JENNIFER: On the second floor is she?

BOB: I live on the second floor. She is on the third.

JENNIFER: Otherwise known as the attic?

BOB: You may borrow any of the books on these shelves in the hall.

JENNIFER: Should I decide to accept the job.

             It's locked.

(Still in the bookstore, ALBERT holds up the key. BOB goes to him, reaching for it.)

(To herself.) Ever so fancy. A fluted glass knob. A nameplate.

(BOB opens the door. JENNIFER shudders. She doesn't look in.)

BOB: What do you think?

JENNIFER: I think a one-room suite is an oxymoron. It sounds small.

BOB: How does it look?

JENNIFER: *(Looking.)* Very...dark and narrow. Who lived here?

BOB: It has been empty many years.

JENNIFER: It's fully furnished.

BOB: Waiting for someone such as yourself.

JENNIFER: Such as myself?

            Who looked after your mother before?

BOB: She looked after herself.

JENNIFER: But now she can't?

BOB: Now she can't.

JENNIFER: Since when?

BOB: Yesterday.

JENNIFER: What happened yesterday?

BOB: Who can tell?

JENNIFER: Was she normal before?

BOB: No, no. Never that. But she looked after herself.

JENNIFER: I had better see her. *(She shudders.)*

BOB: What's your name?

JENNIFER: Jennifer. What's yours?

BOB: Bob.

JENNIFER: Shall we go up?

              Bob?

BOB: Do you consider yourself a brave person Jennifer?

JENNIFER: How brave would I have to be? Will she attack?

BOB: No, no. She does nothing of her own volition.

JENNIFER: Maybe it's only temporary.

BOB: We hadn't thought of that.

JENNIFER: We?

BOB: My father and I. Excuse me. I can't help noticing you shudder every once in a while. Is it the idea of going into the suite?

JENNIFER: What makes you think it would be that?

BOB: Maybe you think it's haunted.

JENNIFER: I don't believe in ghosts.

BOB: Then I won't worry.

JENNIFER: On the other hand, I think you should tell me the truth.

BOB: Yes, I think I should tell you the truth. But I don't believe you'd believe me. Also, I'm afraid you won't take the job.

JENNIFER: Would you like me to take the job?

BOB: Yes.

JENNIFER: Why?

                (The GIRL enters and steps up behind JENNIFER. JENNIFER is unaware of her presence. BOB sees her. Once she is behind JENNIFER, the GIRL peeks out once in a while at BOB.)

BOB: I don't know. You seem competent. And brave. And good.

JENNIFER: That's a generous assessment of a person you've known three minutes. I think you simply want me to be competent and brave and good. It would be a convenience to you.

BOB: And perceptive.

                Please, come in and look at the suite.

                (They enter the room. The GIRL remains behind JENNIFER.)

JENNIFER: It's obvious to anyone—perceptive or not—that this room, this suite as you call it, has not been empty for years.

BOB: In a way it has been.

JENNIFER: There are cornflakes in the cupboard.

BOB: A Nazi lived here.

                Are you afraid?

JENNIFER: How long did he live here?

BOB: All my life. I've spent all my life learning to forgive him.

JENNIFER: I suppose the days seem long now that he's gone.

BOB: He died yesterday.

                What do you think he left me?

                This.

(He shows her a whip.)

JENNIFER: I suppose it would have to be something of that sort.

BOB: Do you know what people say when I show them this?

JENNIFER: It would have to be something of that sort?

BOB: I wish they did say that. I wish everyone was like you.

JENNIFER: You assume too much. That's a sign that you want too much.

BOB: No. No I want nothing. I expect nothing.

JENNIFER: Hah! I could count on my nose the number of times anyone I've met has expected nothing.

BOB: That would be one. One person, to equal one nose. That would be me. I'd be the one.

JENNIFER: You're not lacking in the ego department, are you?

BOB: Not where expecting nothing is concerned.

JENNIFER: What do people say when you show them that?

BOB: They say, "I'd hate to be on the wrong end of that."

JENNIFER: Do they?

BOB: Yes.

JENNIFER: What do you say?

BOB: Nothing. I think about it.

JENNIFER: Do you have a garden?

BOB: She used to garden. It's grown wild now. She stopped looking after it long ago.

JENNIFER: Does "she" refer to your mother?

BOB: Yes. Do you like to garden?

JENNIFER: It might be an antidote.

                Any delphiniums?

BOB: Yes.

JENNIFER: Blue?

BOB: All shades of blue.

JENNIFER: You could bury that in the garden.

                You could cut it into three.

                You could burn it.

BOB: I believe it's worth money. I might need it some-
                day. Maybe to pay your wages.

JENNIFER: Should I accept the job.

BOB: Yes.

JENNIFER: What do you do for money ordinarily?

BOB: I own a second-hand bookstore.

JENNIFER: That sounds innocuous enough.

BOB: We are innocuous. Believe me. It's only that this
                man lived here all these years. We had nothing to
                do with him. I've spent my life forgiving him.

JENNIFER: For crimes you can't understand.

BOB: You understand.

JENNIFER: Please don't assume that.

BOB: I think you do. You might. Understand us, I mean.
                No one would expect you to understand him.

JENNIFER: I have to tell you Bob, of all the worrisome aspects
                of this situation, the most worrisome is your ten-
                dency to assume too much.

BOB: Jennifer, I sense a sweetness in you. Delphiniums.
                Blue. You asked for them. They grow wild in our
                garden. They grow as tall as you. I know I'll see you
                standing among them this summer.

JENNIFER: That depends. Let me see your mother.

                (The GIRL exits.)

                I walked up to a door. I opened it only to find
                another door. I opened it and found another. Door
                after door I went, progressing, I thought, though
                soon I expected only another door. When the last
                door opened, before me was a scene, backed by a
                painted cyclorama. A skinny creek flowed into
                painted grass and painted trees. Along the creek
                was a bike path where a little girl was roller skat-
                ing. Along the bike path, boys and girls and men
                and women leaned over the railings, looking into
                the creek. A television van and another vehicle,
                that had a red light flashing, were parked on real
                grass in front of the cyclorama. Cameramen were
                filming. A diver surfaced in the creek. The little girl
                skated over to the railing. I wasn't the little girl but
                I was bound to her and went wherever she went. A
                boy told her divers were clearing refuse from the
                culverts so the creek could drain. He pointed down
                the creek where a diver was attaching a rope to a
                shopping cart he'd brought up from the bottom.

                A woman came walking along the bike path. She
                stopped at an ice cream cart. The vehicle with the
                red light flashing was an ice cream cart. She bought
                a revel from the ice cream boy. She came over to the
                little girl and held the revel out. The child took the
                ice cream. She skated away.

                I thought: this child represents the child I was, the
                day before I learned to be afraid. Yet that was not
                true because the girl skated back to the railing to
                watch until the divers rose again and I know she
                was thinking they would drag up a body next. It

seemed they must drag up a body sometime or what was living for? With both hands on the railing, she leaned her own small body toward the creek. She lifted her right foot and swung it back and forth so the wheels of her skate spun on the pavement. She waited. On either side of her, all along the bike path, boys and girls and men and women leaned toward the creek, waiting. The child put her right foot down and began spinning the wheels of her left skate, waiting to see who they'd dredge up, if it would be her mother.

(A blackboard on an easel appears. On it is written: "Our Theory of Goodness".)

ALBERT: "Some enchanted evening—"

BOB: What's up Dad? What's with the blackboard?

Dad?

"Our Theory of Goodness"?

Is this supposed to be a message for Jennifer?

(ALBERT nods.)

I don't know Dad. It seems a bit blatant. You think it's necessary?

(ALBERT nods.)

I thought things were going okay.

(ALBERT shakes his head.)

She's a naturally good person.

(ALBERT shakes his head.

MARIE enters. She sits like a Henry Moore sculpture, utterly immobile and seemingly unmovable, on a park bench. She remains detached from everything that happens. Occasionally she changes position and takes up another statue-like pose.

ALBERT sticks his head in his bag.)

JENNIFER: You should be ashamed of yourself.

ALBERT: I like my balls.

JENNIFER: A grown man.

(*She indicates the blackboard.*) What's this? "Our Theory of Goodness".

Bob, did you notice that you and your father use a number of words that aren't in common currency?

BOB: We've had to.

ALBERT: Living with a Nazi, it takes its toll on you.

I wonder how she'll sleep.

JENNIFER: You wonder how I'll sleep?

ALBERT: In the Nazi's bed.

JENNIFER: It's my bed now.

Should I choose to stay.

BOB: What do people talk about now? The people who don't talk about goodness.

JENNIFER: You don't have the slightest interest in what people talk about now.

BOB: No, I'd like to know.

JENNIFER: I don't know.

ALBERT: I think she knows.

(*JENNIFER goes to the blackboard and writes "Our Theory for Success".)*

BOB: "Our Theory for Success".

ALBERT: Bob doesn't try to be successful.

JENNIFER: He tries to be good.

ALBERT: Yes.

JENNIFER: And you try to be good.

ALBERT: Yes.

JENNIFER: You'll never get anywhere that way you know.

Look. You know what the main difference is between these two headings?

The main difference is this. (*She circles the "for" and "of".*)

"Of". "Theory of"." Indicates the status quo. People who are satisfied use the word "of". People who are satisfied with just being.

"For" is proactive. "For" is goal-oriented. A theory "for" looks forward—into the future. "For" is for people who want things and try to get them.

ALBERT: There's a difference between "Goodness" and "Success" too.

JENNIFER: Yes. One's from the Dark Ages, the other is appropriate in today's world. One's from a cave dweller's perspective, the other's realistic.

(*Giving in to him.*) One's about you, the other's about me.

ALBERT: That's right.

JENNIFER: You've got to start with yourself.

BOB: "To thine own self be true."

JENNIFER: If you want to put it archaically.

(*JENNIFER turns her back on the others.*)

BOB: She didn't mean all that about success. Just the opposite I suspect. She wouldn't be here looking after a woman who can't look after herself if she knew the first thing about success. I believe she was being ironic.

ALBERT: It's dangerous having a woman like that in the house.

BOB: She was the only one who applied for the job Dad. I think she'll stay on.

ALBERT: I didn't want to tell you Bob.

                   I saw her pushing your mother around.

                   In the park. Your mother didn't want to get up off the bench. She shoved her Bob. I don't think we can have that.

BOB: It can't be an easy job.

                   I'll try something else. I'll explain it to her Dad. I think we could all be happy together.

                   (ALBERT sticks his head into his bag.

                   The light dims to near darkness.)

                   Ladies and gentlemen—

JENNIFER: —Gentleman.

                   There's only one.

                   Even that is highly dubious.

ALBERT: I wonder if I've been offended?

BOB: Ladies and gentleman—

ALBERT: —Excuse me? I'd like to know if I've been offended.

JENNIFER: If you don't know, you haven't been.

ALBERT: It's hard to know, with you.

JENNIFER: You don't know me.

BOB: Ladies and—

ALBERT: —You live with someone, you'd think you'd know them. You'd think you could trust them.

BOB: Excuse me—

JENNIFER: —That's an insult.

BOB: Excuse me—?

JENNIFER: —Take it back.

ALBERT: I never insult anyone. Bob, do I ever—

BOB: —Wait a minute. Is anyone interested in this experiment?

ALBERT: Sorry Bob.

JENNIFER: Sorry Bob.

ALBERT: Start again, would you Bob?

BOB: Ladies and gentlemen: we have gathered to witness—

JENNIFER: —Man.

BOB: I'm including myself, Jennifer. I know I'm performing the experiment, but I'm a watcher too. Because I've never done it before. So, ladies and gentlemen: we have gathered to witness an experiment. The embodiment of an Idea. We have before us a sheet of tinfoil. It's been crumpled and then flattened out to simulate the pier-glass or polished steel referred to in George Eliot's novel, *Middlemarch*. We have examined the tinfoil. We have noted that its surface is covered with minute lines like the scratches on a polished steel surface and we have agreed that the lines go every which way. They form no pattern. Also we have agreed to think of the lines as events.

JENNIFER: I'm not sure I can agree to that.

ALBERT: You already agreed.

JENNIFER: I'm thinking of changing my mind.

ALBERT: Why?

BOB: Is there something wrong with the analogy Jennifer?

JENNIFER: It's vague.

BOB: Okay.

JENNIFER: It's vague and arbitrary.

ALBERT: She just wants to argue.

BOB: Vague and arbitrary.

ALBERT: We agreed that the lines are like events, things that happen in life.

JENNIFER: When? Where? And who to?

ALBERT: To whom.

            Well, she's always correcting everybody.

BOB: I think we agreed to think of the lines as events because that's what George Eliot tells us to do, and if we want to see how her analogy works, we have to follow her directions.

JENNIFER: Fine. Just go on with it then.

BOB: We don't have to be so vague though. We could narrow it down to events this year, or today…

JENNIFER: Where?

ALBERT: Wherever you want.

JENNIFER: Thank you Albert. How about this city?

BOB: Okay. This sheet of tinfoil represents—this city. Each line on the foil represents an event that is happening—right now—in this city, to the citizens of this city.

ALBERT: That's neat Bob.

JENNIFER: Does that include us?

ALBERT: Of course it includes us.

BOB: And we've agreed, have we? That the lines are random? They go all over the place? There's no pattern to them?

JENNIFER: Yes.

ALBERT: Agreed.

BOB: Then I will light a candle.

              (BOB lights a candle.)

              We have agreed, too, that the candle is to represent our selves?

ALBERT: One self. One candle can only represent one self. Just thought I'd say that before Jennifer did.

JENNIFER: I wish I could think of my self even as steady as a candle flame.

BOB: One self. The egoism, as George Eliot says, of any person.

              (BOB places the candle on the foil sheet. JENNIFER and ALBERT come closer to look.)

ALBERT: I can't say I notice anything Bob.

BOB: No. But wait—Yes, it is like she says. Look closer. Within the candle's light, the lines do seem to arrange themselves in circles.

ALBERT: I guess so.

JENNIFER: Blow it out and light it again.

                   Yes, it's true, if you look closely.

BOB: It's an illusion of course. By illuminating some of the lines and excluding others, the candle creates the illusion of a pattern of circles, radiating outward from its centre. Just as the ego produces the flattering illusion of its self at the centre of events.

ALBERT: Right here, right now, in this city…

JENNIFER: In this room…

ALBERT: Each one of us…

BOB: That's right. And. It's not enough to realize that you think of yourself as the centre of events that in reality don't centre around you. You have to remember that everyone else thinks of themselves the same way.

                   (BOB lights three other candles while he talks and places them in a row on the foil.)

ALBERT: Now there's a row of circles. That's neat Bob.

JENNIFER: What's it prove?

BOB: It doesn't prove anything. It's just a demonstration—of a way of thinking.

JENNIFER: What's it supposed to prove?

                   What's it supposed to prove Bob?

BOB: I just wanted us to think about it Jennifer.

JENNIFER: Us.

BOB: All of us.

JENNIFER: You hear that Marie?

I don't think your mother gets it Bob. You get it do you Albert?

ALBERT: Bob's just trying to help.

JENNIFER: Our Theory of Goodness, is it?

BOB: Wait. Look.

(BOB moves the candles so they stand very close together.)

We can gather the circles together, almost like one light.

So maybe it's possible to share a perspective? To create a circle other people would want to share?

(JENNIFER blows out her candle. The others blow out the remaining candles. ALBERT puts his head in his bag. BOB stands in a corner like a child being punished.

JENNIFER's dream, suffused with a glassy bright light, begins. Music is playing, a soft Chopin or similar piano sonata.)

JENNIFER: *(Off.)* Come out to the veranda.

(The GIRL enters, dressed in a Victorian costume and entirely in white. She wears her hair in one long braid down her back.)

GIRL: Ooo. It's all glass. Look. Even the doors are glass.

JENNIFER: Yes, and see? The roof too.

GIRL: The roof, the walls, the door. It's like a glass house.

JENNIFER: I knew you'd like it.

GIRL: You can see the trees and into the sky. It's so... Is someone playing the piano?

JENNIFER: Someone very far away, in time as well as place. It's a recording.

GIRL: It's very pretty. Thank you for bringing me here. You are looking after me so well.

JENNIFER: I like to look after you well.

GIRL: Will you fix my hair?

JENNIFER: If you wish, I will fix your hair, as you say.

GIRL: You see, it's coming loose.

               (The GIRL stands before JENNIFER, who begins undoing the braid at the bottom. The bottom half of the GIRL's hair comes off in JENNIFER's hands. Her hair has been broken at shoulder level. It had been skillfully woven together into the braid. JENNIFER holds the hair in her hands, astonished and not wanting the girl to know.)

JENNIFER: Who braided your hair before?

GIRL: My mother.

JENNIFER: I will try to do it as well as she did.

GIRL: Oh I'm sure you can do as well.

               (JENNIFER works to put the braid back together and is succeeding when there is a knock on the glass door.)

JENNIFER: Was that someone knocking?

               (Lightning flashes.)

GIRL: It must have been thunder.

               (JENNIFER resumes her task. After a minute, the knocking resumes, but this time it is violent.)

JENNIFER: *(Calling.)* Who are you?

               (The glass is rattled violently. JENNIFER stands between the GIRL and the door.)

               Go away. Please. Go away.

(A brilliant flash of lightning is followed by a loud clap of thunder and more knocking. JENNIFER pulls the GIRL away from the door and they exit.

The piano sonata continues while the light shifts. Then the music fades away.

JENNIFER enters and sits with MARIE on the park bench. JENNIFER rises and takes MARIE's hand. MARIE doesn't respond. She remains as a statue. JENNIFER tugs. No response.)

It's time to go.

Come on.

Fuck.

I mean it Marie, it's time to go.

(JENNIFER tries to shove MARIE off the bench.)

Fuck.

(JENNIFER pushes MARIE hard, then hits her when she doesn't respond. Then sits down, giving up. ALBERT sits beside them and puts his face into his bag.)

ALBERT: *(Sings wistfully.)* "Some enchanted evening—Some enchanted evening—"

JENNIFER: Must you?

ALBERT: Sorry.

            Did you have your nap?

            How did you sleep in the Nazi's bed?

JENNIFER: It's my bed now.

ALBERT: I'm remembering the woman who cried.

JENNIFER: What woman?

ALBERT: A woman came into the bookstore and cried.

               Mesmerizing, she was. When she walked into the store and stood there in that sunlight. The door closed slowly, and it was like the sunlight pulled away from her.

               She wanted a book Bob didn't have.

               (At the mention of his name, BOB turns to them and waits with his hand out.)

JENNIFER: And cried when she couldn't have it? Sounds like a big fuss over nothing.

ALBERT: You don't understand.

JENNIFER: And you do?

ALBERT: Yes. I understand.

               I am a watcher.

               I am a thinker.

               I am a student of human behaviour.

JENNIFER: Well I'm not. There isn't enough time in the day.

ALBERT: You could imagine her. The woman who cried. You could imagine being her.

JENNIFER: Know what? I'd rather imagine being you.

               Quite a concept isn't it? It couldn't be all that hard.

               I'm a watcher.

               I'm a thinker.

               I'm a student of human behaviour.

ALBERT: Okay, be me when she came into the store.

JENNIFER: Where am I?

               On my usual chair in the corner?

ALBERT: Yes.

JENNIFER: With my head in my bag?

ALBERT: More or less.

JENNIFER: More or less. More or less nuzzling my balls?

ALBERT: Sure.

JENNIFER: How do I feel?

ALBERT: Pretty good. You feel pretty good. You know, it's a pretty nice morning. Sun coming in the window. The store window's dusty and streaked, hasn't been cleaned since fall and you're sitting there thinking—

JENNIFER: —about how Bob will have to clean that window.

ALBERT: That's right Jennifer.

JENNIFER: God you're lazy. Where is Bob?

ALBERT: Bob's in the basement, unpacking books. He hasn't had a customer all morning.

JENNIFER: Kind of a slow morning for a student of human behaviour.

ALBERT: Yeah. But you're comfortable sitting there, just you and the dust motes.

JENNIFER: And the smell of old books and old wood.

ALBERT: Yeah. Your song starts sneaking up your spine—

JENNIFER: —You should be ashamed. You should be embarrassed to talk like that.

             Bad enough you sing that dumb song all the time.

ALBERT: I'm just trying to describe what it's like being me.

JENNIFER: Okay so I'm singing.

ALBERT: No, not yet. You're just feeling the song start. Okay? It starts down low in your spine, a kind of buzzing feeling, and it works its way up. You can feel it before you even think of the words or the tune. You can feel it moving up and when it gets to the back of your neck it feels like someone's hand brushing your hair up onto your head, you know? Kind of a numb feeling and kind of tingly too and you know any second the words and the tune are going to flush into your brain, any second now, and when it does, it's going to come bursting out of you.

I consider it a coincidence that I was singing that song just before the woman who cried came into the store.

JENNIFER: A coincidence?

ALBERT: It's a romantic song. And it was romantic. She was. It was romantic. Jennifer.

JENNIFER: You don't know the meaning of the word. Anyway, it was hardly a coincidence. You always sing that song.

ALBERT: I'm getting ahead of myself. You're sitting letting your song slide up your spine when you hear Bob coming up the stairs. Try to feel it again, the song, feel it kind of sneaking up, building…

JENNIFER: You should hear yourself.

ALBERT: I enjoy myself.

JENNIFER: You have no conception of yourself in a real world.

ALBERT: On the contrary—

JENNIFER: *(Finishing his sentence.)* —You're a student of yourself in a real world.

Anyway, I'm being you. Any minute now my song's going to bust out all over.

ALBERT: That's right. As soon as Bob opens the basement
             door.

JENNIFER: You'll have to be Bob.

ALBERT: Oh, no, that's okay.

JENNIFER: I have to be you.

ALBERT: You don't have to.

JENNIFER: I'm willing to.

ALBERT: It's easy being me. You just have to sit there.

JENNIFER: At least I'm trying.

ALBERT: You know what Jennifer? It's really nice of you.

             (BOB approaches them.)

             Bob! Be you.

BOB: Say that again?

JENNIFER: Albert can't imagine being you.

ALBERT: The day the woman who cried came into the store,
             you came up the stairs with the radio. They were
             playing Tchaikovsky. A piano concerto. Wait a
             minute.

             (ALBERT pulls a tape recorder out of a pocket.)

BOB: How is she? *(Meaning MARIE.)*

JENNIFER: Same as ever.

             *(ALBERT plays a scrap of Tchaikovsky's "Piano
             Concerto No. 1".)*

BOB: Jennifer? The job's not too much for you?

JENNIFER: No.

             (He turns it off and rewinds the tape.)

ALBERT: We're set. Come on.

BOB: Come on what?

ALBERT: Jennifer's going to be me, I'll be you, and you can
             be the woman who cried.

             Come on. I want to show Jennifer.

             Jennifer, you ready?

             *(JENNIFER picks up ALBERT's bag, opens it and
             sticks her head inside. ALBERT gives BOB the tape
             deck.)*

             (To JENNIFER.) You're nearly ready to sing.

             (To BOB.) You're just going to open the door and
             come in with the radio playing.

BOB: No, no, no. You're me.

ALBERT: Right.

             *(ALBERT turns on the Tchaikovsky. He motions to
             JENNIFER to begin. His right hand sways to the
             music. He imitates BOB marching joyfully up and
             down the aisles of the bookstore, led by his hand.)*

JENNIFER: *(Sings.)* "Some enchanted evening— Some en-
             chanted evening—"

             Now what?

ALBERT: Go to the window and say, "Excuse me Bob."

JENNIFER: Excuse me Bob.

ALBERT: Of course Dad. Everyone is excused. Here. Not out
             there. Wouldn't be practical, would it? But here,
             we are all excused.

             *(Carried away, ALBERT takes over both parts of the
             conversation, playing both himself and BOB.)*

             – I think you're going to have a customer.

That would be a novelty.

– I'm not sure… I think she's coming this way.

You're in danger of raising my hopes Dad.

– I do see a woman Bob. Would you say your hopes are raised?

I'm not sure Dad.

– If you're not sure, they aren't.

They might be.

– She is definitely walking this way Bob.

Probably going to the shoe repair.

– No, I think she's coming here.

She's carrying something. Isn't it shoes?

– It's fish. She came out of the fish store. She's clutching a fish!

Clutching a fish?

– Clutching a fish. It could be a lobster.

It could be a squid.

– A-a-a-a-a!

(To BOB.) Tell her what it was like.

A woman came into the store…

BOB:	A woman came into the store…
ALBERT:	Clutching…
BOB:	Clutching a fish…
ALBERT:	Wrapped in brown paper. Describe her.
BOB:	She had brown hair.

ALBERT: And a body like a bolster.

JENNIFER: A bolster!

ALBERT: I mean straight and solid.

BOB: Her body with the light behind it was a lovely, solid thing.

              (When BOB says "book about a young girl", MARIE rises and walks off. The others don't notice.)

              She asked for a book about a young girl who grows up in the Everglades or some place like that and collects moths and her mother is mean to her. I said that would be *A Girl of the Limberlost*.

ALBERT: She said: Yes. I loved it when I was a girl. And Bob said: Unfortunately I haven't got a copy. And I'm afraid it's out of print so you'll have some difficulty finding it.

BOB: I said: I could make a note of your name. If we happen to get one second-hand, I could call you.

ALBERT: She said: I wanted it today.

BOB: She started to cry. I didn't know what to say.

ALBERT: There isn't much a guy can do to stop a woman crying.

JENNIFER: Where's Marie?

              Where's Marie?

              (BOB and ALBERT exchange looks.)

BOB: Don't worry Jennifer. You'll find her.

ALBERT: Where were we?

BOB: I asked if she'd tried the library. She said she was sorry; it was silly to cry over a book.

ALBERT: You'll find that book Bob. You'll find it for her.

BOB: It's only a book.

ALBERT: Know what Bob? She really wants this book. You're going to find it. And it will make her happy.

(A glassy cold light that can splinter and shift.

JENNIFER's mother, played by MARIE, appears at one end of a long table. Nearby is ALBERT's blackboard. A scientific-looking formula is written on it. JENNIFER puts on a white lab coat.)

JENNIFER: Last night in my dream I had a terrible fight with my mother. But this reminds me of another dream. I was a young woman—scientist—in a white coat. I was reading a complicated formula on a blackboard and stepped forward and amended it by adding a mathematical sentence which stood for a new element or chemical.

I stepped back and looked at the formula as it now read. Suddenly an older woman, also in a white lab coat, appeared beside me. I knew I'd made a huge error. A catastrophic explosion was about to occur. I cried out: "Mother, I've split apart."

(JENNIFER walks to the end of the table opposite her mother.)

Did you say something? I thought you said something sharp to me.

Mother...?

If you're angry why don't you speak?

(Her mother is extremely angry. She grabs a wine glass, puts the base into her mouth, chomps it off with her teeth and begins chewing it.)

(So enraged she can barely whisper.) If you ever do that again, I will leave this house.

(Her mother bites into the glass again. JENNIFER removes her lab coat and tosses it aside.)

BOB: You're not leaving?

JENNIFER: I tried it. It's not for me.

BOB: It was too much for you?

ALBERT: She's afraid to sleep in that bed.

JENNIFER: I have a job, a home and a husband.

I'd have to be a different person to live here.

BOB: If you'll leave your address—

JENNIFER: No.

BOB: I'll find the book—

JENNIFER: Thank you but it was a desire of the moment and the time has passed. I no longer want the book.

(JENNIFER exits. After a moment, BOB follows his hand after her. ALBERT sticks his head into his bag. MARIE remains frozen. The GIRL sneaks on, keeping her distance from MARIE. She pulls on JENNIFER's discarded lab coat. She goes to the blackboard, picks up the chalk and starts to print. After she has printed the letter "I" the blackboard pulls away from her and disappears.)

GIRL: I will not take candy from strangers. I will not take candy from strangers. I promise I won't let anyone hurt me.

(To MARIE.) If I am very good, you'll get better.

(All exit.)

Part Two

(JENNIFER's house.

An urban backyard with trees and a deck. JENNIFER stands on the deck, looking out. She is wearing only a long cotton shirt. Her hair is wet.

During this scene, the watery light of a long summer evening dims gradually to darkness. It begins green and sensual and restless, with the branches of the trees lifting and falling.)

DAVID: *(Off.)* Jennifer? Where are you?

Jennifer, I don't see any wine here.

Where are you?

JENNIFER: I'm here.

DAVID: Jennifer?

JENNIFER: Here.

(DAVID comes out on the deck.)

DAVID: Oh there you are. Where's the wine? I don't see any wine. Jennifer? It's not in the fridge.

JENNIFER: I forgot.

DAVID: You forgot?

JENNIFER: People will bring wine.

DAVID: It won't be cold. I phoned you to remind you.

JENNIFER: *(Remembering.)* I wanted to tell you something, when you phoned—David, I saw a man today, walking down the sidewalk—

DAVID: —You saw a man today. Jennifer, we don't have time for this. You said you'd get the wine. You said you'd clean the house. You had the day off work. The house is a mess Jennifer. Your hair's wet.

I'm not going to talk about the wine, or the house. Your hair's wet.

It's seven o'clock. It's seven o'clock. Our guests are due to arrive. You're not dressed.

Did you make the salad?

ANNE: *(Off, gaily.)* Anybody home?

> *(JENNIFER goes into the house. ANNE and JOHN enter. JOHN is carrying a bottle of wine.)*

DAVID: Hey guys. Good to see you. John, Anne.

ANNE: Hello David. Lovely evening for this.

JOHN: Wine.

DAVID: Thanks.

ANNE: It's not cold.

DAVID: What'll you have to drink? Anne?

ANNE: I'll have wine. White please.

JOHN: How about a beer?

DAVID: Beer's in the cooler.

ANNE: Isn't this nice?

DAVID: Have a chair Anne.

ANNE: It's so lovely to sit under the trees. Or does the hostess need help?

(JENNIFER comes out, dressed.)

JENNIFER: *(Echoing.)* It's so lovely to sit under the trees.

ANNE: Oh hello Jennifer.

JENNIFER: Hello Anne.

ANNE: Can I help you with anything?

JENNIFER: Go and sit.

ANNE: I'm happy to help.

JENNIFER: Sit under the trees Anne.

(JENNIFER goes inside.)

DAVID: Can I get you a drink Anne?

ANNE: You asked me already.

DAVID: Sorry.

JOHN: Hey, it's not easy being the perfect host.

DAVID: White wine, right?

ANNE: I'd love some. Such a perfect evening for a barbe-cue. Such a good idea, David.

DAVID: I'll get that drink.

(DAVID goes inside with the wine. The following conversation between DAVID and JENNIFER takes place offstage and can be heard by ANNE and JOHN.)

(Off.) This isn't cold. Anne would like a glass of cold wine.

JENNIFER: What's that poem? About the trees? The trees bending...

(ANNE and JOHN respond to this poetic conversation by replacing themselves —by putting

cardboard silhouettes on their chairs—or they stand and are replaced with their silhouettes. They exit.)

Stick an ice cube in her glass.

DAVID: Stick an ice cube in her glass.

JENNIFER: Yes.

DAVID: Bring her a glass of wine with ice in it?

JENNIFER: Just put it in for a minute, then fish it out.

(JOHN and ANNE enter the yard and wait by the deck. ANNE is carrying a bottle of wine.)

When the trees bow down their heads... No, that's not it. Girls. The trees...like girls bending to dry their hair.

(DAVID comes out.)

ANNE: There's our host.

DAVID: Anne. John. Good to see you.

JOHN: How's it going David?

DAVID: Good, good. How are you two?

ANNE: We're fine.

DAVID: Come on over. You know these two.

JOHN: Sure. How's things?

DAVID: Can I get you a drink?

ANNE: I'd love a glass of wine, white please. Here. It isn't cold.

DAVID: No problem.

ANNE: Isn't your yard lovely? All these trees.

DAVID: Help yourself to a beer John.

(DAVID puts on a tape of Lester Young and the Piano Giants: "I Guess I'll Have to Change My Plan". Then he goes inside. The following conversation between DAVID and JENNIFER is offstage, and can be heard by the others.)

Jennifer. Where are you?

JENNIFER: Here.

DAVID: Did you remember the fish? You know Anne doesn't eat red meat.

JENNIFER: Oh, the fish.

DAVID: What do you mean, "Oh, the fish."

JENNIFER: I'm afraid I left it in the car all afternoon.

(ANNE and JOHN replace themselves with cardboard figures. They exit.)

DAVID: Did you make the salad?

JENNIFER: I'm making it.

DAVID: Now?

JENNIFER: Yes.

DAVID: I don't see any evidence of that. Are you planning to spend the evening in the kitchen, Jennifer?

(ANNE and JOHN enter. She is carrying a pizza pan and he has a bottle of wine. DAVID comes out.)

Anne! John! You made it. Great.

JOHN: Hi, David.

ANNE: Where's Jennifer?

DAVID: In the kitchen.

ANNE: I'll see if she needs help.

JENNIFER: (*Off.*) I'm better off on my own thanks Anne.

ANNE: I've brought a vegetable appetizer pizza.

DAVID: Great. We can have it now. We're a little behind. Come on over. Meet the others. I don't think you know everyone.

ANNE: No. But it's so nice to see new faces.

JENNIFER: (*Off.*) So lovely to sit under trees.

DAVID: Help yourself to a beer John. What'll you have Anne?

ANNE: White wine please.

DAVID: I keep forgetting the wine. Damn.

JOHN: Hey, it's not easy being the perfect host.

    (*DAVID goes into the house.*)

ANNE: (*To a guest.*) Isn't this nice? Are your children interested in the environment?

JOHN: It's a good idea to have a barbecue.

ANNE: It's so nice to get together.

JOHN: Makes you feel part of a community.

    (*DAVID and JENNIFER's conversation offstage can be heard by the others.*)

DAVID: Where are the salad things? Jennifer?

ANNE: It's a beautiful yard. And the weather—

DAVID: (*Reminding her.*) Lettuce. Lemons. Oil. Egg.

    (*ANNE jumps to her feet and begins to pass her tray around.*)

ANNE: Have some of this. It's called vegetable appetizer pizza.

DAVID: Garlic. Anchovies. Parmesan. Croutons.

ANNE: It's so easy. You use that Pillsbury dough. A secret ingredient. And any vegetables you like. *(Turning to another guest.)* Your daughter won the centennial medal. I saw her.

(DAVID hurries out with wine and glasses.)

Thank you David. *(To another guest.)* Are you the ones on Laurier who just put in the pool? I envy you. Our son is a swimmer. I suggested to John last year that we should put in a lap pool but Jamie said it wouldn't be good enough for practising. But just to be able to sit by the water, jump in when it's hot.

JENNIFER: *(Off.)* Our son is a swimmer. Your daughter won a medal.

JOHN: The Thompsons on the corner of Laurier are adding a sunroom to their house. A thousand square feet.

ANNE: Isn't it a wonderful evening? Do you golf? We did eighteen this morning and it got so hot I thought I'd die. But it's beautiful this evening in the shade.

JOHN: There's a breeze.

ANNE: I don't feel a breeze.

JOHN: We're sheltered here. But look at the tops of the trees.

ANNE: Beautiful trees. How's work going David?

DAVID: Fine. Good.

Guess I'd better fire up the barbie.

JOHN: Want some help David?

DAVID: Sure John.

JOHN: I'll open us a couple of beers.

ANNE: *(Calling.)* Come sit with us, Jennifer. You're going
                 to far too much trouble tonight.

                 *(A wedge-shaped shadow appears at the corner of
                 the yard, near the deck, stage left. JENNIFER comes
                 out to the deck. BOB appears in the shadow at the
                 corner of the yard. He stands unseen by the others,
                 watching them, his right arm raised and stretched
                 tentatively toward them.)*

JENNIFER: Thanks Anne. Yes, I'll get the salad. The salad is my
                 responsibility, you know. The men tend the barbe-
                 cues. The women make the salads.

ANNE: And vegetable appetizer pizza.

JENNIFER: Definitely. Just as violent—all that chopping and
                 tearing—but the vegetables are nicer, aren't they
                 Anne? They don't bleed like meat. What are we
                 sacrificing tonight guys?

JOHN: A cow!

ANNE: John really.

DAVID: We're having steaks.

                 *(JENNIFER goes inside, then comes out with the
                 salad.)*

JOHN: *(Seeing BOB.)* Hey. Come on over. Pull up a chair.

                 *(BOB walks into the yard, following his hand. He
                 must follow his hand; his entire body turns wher-
                 ever it points. He uses his left hand to steer himself,
                 but he is unable to proceed in any direction for long.
                 It's impossible to guess what his goal is though he
                 seems to have one. DAVID goes to meet him but
                 BOB's path is so erratic, they can't meet. DAVID
                 gets frustrated, but BOB reacts to his problem with
                 humble self-mockery. Whenever he gets close to the
                 others, BOB greets them by offering to shake hands
                 or hug, nodding, bowing, or tipping an imaginary
                 cap.)*

ANNE: John?

JOHN: Do they know this guy?

ANNE: I don't think they do.

JENNIFER: But how nice to see new faces.

             *(BOB lurches past DAVID who is left facing
             JENNIFER. DAVID has heard her and turns from
             her, disgusted. JOHN traps BOB momentarily,
             though without touching him. BOB looks fright-
             ened. JENNIFER, watching, is frightened.)*

JOHN: *(To BOB.)* Hey. Hey, now. That's enough of that.

             (DAVID intervenes.)

DAVID: *(To BOB, kindly.)* Can I help you?

             (BOB moves away to the edge of the lawn.)

ANNE: I think I've seen him before, in the library down-
             town. You know how they hang out there? Those
             people?

JOHN: Ignore him. He'll go away.

             *(DAVID and JENNIFER join their guests. BOB
             immediately comes back and circles them, pointing
             at them.)*

             Ignore him.

             (They all pretend to be ignoring him.)

ANNE: *(After a moment.)* What's new with you Jennifer?

JENNIFER: Not much. What's new with you Anne?

ANNE: Not much either, I guess.

JOHN: You went golfing today.

ANNE: Yes.

JOHN: You did eighteen. Jennifer, I'm sure you did at least eighteen things today…

JENNIFER: *(Looking at BOB.)* I can't remember.

               (The guests look apprehensively at BOB, who is still circling them.)

DAVID: I'm sorry about this…

JENNIFER: *(To BOB.)* Won't you sit with us?

               (Appealing to ANNE.) Anne, have you ever been in that sculpture room in the art gallery? Once I found myself there, alone. All alone in this big room surrounded by these strange sad forms. They reminded me of human bones, of human dinosaurs. When I walked among them, I felt I was mourning. But I could see they were the bones of people who had for a time endured. They were huge and they made me bigger.

DAVID: Jennifer…

JENNIFER: Is the meat ready?

DAVID: Not yet. Is the salad made?

JENNIFER: Yes.

ANNE: I wonder if we shouldn't call someone.

DAVID: *(Going to BOB.)* Can we call someone for you?

ANNE: There must be some agency that would come and pick him up.

JENNIFER: More wine. Anne? How about some supper? Aren't you all hungry? I think we should eat. The meat must be ready.

               (BOB begins to march, his feet lifted high and brought smartly down.)

DAVID: Jesus. I've had it.

JOHN: Call the police.

JENNIFER: Put on some quiet music. He'll calm down. Where's the wine? I'll get more wine. It's a party.

                 (JENNIFER gets the wine.)

ANNE: I suppose he'll go away.

JENNIFER: Here's the salad. Here's the wine. Fill your glasses. Fill your plates. It's a party.

                 Eat, eat.

                 (No one moves. JENNIFER tries to follow BOB. DAVID puts on a tape. Beethoven's Sixth [Pastoral] Symphony, Third Movement "Merry Gathering of Country Folk".)

                 What would you like? Would you like some salad?

                 (BOB starts dancing, adapting to the music. The yard is getting darker.)

ANNE: What is that? Is that the Pastoral Symphony?

JENNIFER: *(Listening.)* I think it's the sound of my husband mocking me.

                 (BOB dances around them. ANNE and JOHN rise to leave.)

                 Don't go. Please don't go. Let's dance. It's getting dark. I'll light some candles.

                 (She lights candles, just a few, far apart.)

                 How lovely the music is. How lovely the trees. Wouldn't you like to dance under the trees, in the twilight, in the breeze? Don't go.

                 (ANNE and JOHN start to gather the cardboard figures. JENNIFER takes one and dances with it. ANNE takes the figure away.)

Don't go Anne. It's a party.

ANNE: *(To DAVID.)* I advise you to call someone.

JOHN: *(To BOB.)* Hey buddy. Time to go home.

JENNIFER: Don't go. It's the music. He likes it. Don't you?

             (BOB stops and faces her. He sidles away, frightened by her volatility.)

I'm starving. Please, sit down. You haven't eaten.

(They all sit. BOB climbs up the tree.)

JENNIFER: Isn't the meat ready?

DAVID: The meat is fucking raw.

JENNIFER: That music. *(Listening.)* The more tender it gets, the harder it is to listen.

             (The sky gets darker. The others huddle into their chairs.)

We're smaller in the night, more like the people we might have been, and more like those we might become.

(Alarmed by this kind of talk, ANNE and JOHN rise.)

It's the music. The music knows more about our lives than we know.

(JOHN and ANNE pick up the figures and leave. The music rises. As JENNIFER continues, the storm sequence, Part Four, begins.)

We'll all be bones some day. As obsolete as dinosaurs. Imagine this yard submerged in water. Our bones floating along the grass like the leaves floating on the breeze. We will all be bones. The square footage of our houses and the scores of our golf games and the trophies our children bring

home will not matter. We should concern our-
selves with bigger things.

(*DAVID ignores her. He begins cleaning up.*)

It's wrong to judge them on their dinner party conversation. But I'm sick of never hearing anything
else. I would rather be alone than be with them.

Our bones are fragile. That's what the music says.
Our thoughts are weak. Our passions puny. Our
souls scrabble on the ground in the dust and dead
leaves.

Or are we too light? We rise too easily to the surface. We should be heavier, stronger.

We should work harder, climb steadily, and not
look back. We should have passions. We should
dare something, risk something, strive for something. We should try to be bigger than we are. We
should want to leave something behind for others
to see.

(*DAVID turns the music off and continues his
cleaning up. The yard is very still.*)

We have no passion, no greatness, no anger or real
love. We want only to do what others have done
and not be embarrassed, not be revealed for what
we are. We want to live undisturbed by strangers.
We want to meet only the strangers who do not
disturb, only those who are not really strangers at
all because they are just like us, followers after the
same followers.

(*To DAVID.*) I hate your cleaning up.

(*DAVID faces her. JENNIFER can't think what to
say. DAVID goes inside. JENNIFER watches him
go, then takes a chair and sits facing the tree BOB
has climbed.*)

(*To BOB.*) I saw you on the street this morning. I watched you walk down the sidewalk. Funny, I watched you through the car window, as though I couldn't be seen myself. But of course you saw me too. You must have seen me too, and followed me home.

How lovely the trees. Tonight, when you came into the yard, only the trees moved, swaying in the breeze, submerged in light.

I love my husband. When he was kind to you, I thought: I will keep this. His kindness.

Then the music. It was so out of place and yet so apt. I wished I could join you. Dance over the grass under the trees. I wished we could all get up off our cheap plastic lawn chairs and dance in the twilight under the trees, sway with the music and cry.

It ended too soon. Too soon. And not enough. Too much village festival and shepherd's song. Not enough storm.

He won't fight. I watched him walking away from me, across the grass, up the steps, away from me. I knew he wasn't going to turn around. I knew he wouldn't come back and talk to me.

> (*Lights down.*
>
> *Morning. An opalescent light.*
>
> *JENNIFER is sleeping in the lawn chair. BOB is still in the tree. DAVID comes out of the house carrying his briefcase.*)

DAVID: Jennifer. Wake up.

> (*DAVID goes to the tree, shakes it. BOB sticks his right hand down tentatively.*)

Time to hit the trail buddy.

JENNIFER: Are you going to work? Would you call Marjorie for me? Tell her I won't be in?

            (DAVID shakes the tree again. BOB climbs down.)

            Time for you to head home, fella.

            (DAVID takes BOB's arm, leads him away, points.)

JENNIFER: David?

DAVID: Go to bed. I'll call Marjorie. Come on pal.

            (BOB goes only as far as DAVID takes him.)

            Okay. I'm going to take you downtown with me. Right downtown. Heart of the city. Where you've got options. Right?

            (DAVID tries to lead BOB off. BOB breaks away. DAVID exits.

            An early evening rippling light descends. JENNIFER pours two glasses of wine and holds one out for BOB.)

JENNIFER: *(Mid-sentence.)* the last light of a summer evening, how it ripples, you know, it enters the yards and runs in the streets slantwise, ripples like a river through the suburbs.

            I think I hear children. Do you hear them? On a summer evening the voices of children sound lonely. They call to one another as though across great distances.

            (BOB returns to her. DAVID enters.)

DAVID: What's going on here—

JENNIFER: Oh David, he came back. When I woke up, he was here.

DAVID: —I told him to go home. *(To BOB.)* I told you to go home. Didn't I tell you that?

JENNIFER: But David—

DAVID: —Jennifer, I'm not having this. Get rid of him. Now.

              (DAVID goes inside.)

JENNIFER: *(Quietly, to BOB.)* Do you think we could meet somewhere else, tomorrow? Maybe for lunch? I could buy you lunch?

              (DAVID sticks his head out.)

DAVID: I'm going to nuke a couple of pieces of steak for supper. Remember? The leftover steak from last night? The steak that wasn't eaten because our bar-becue turned into a fiasco? Two pieces. I'm nuking two pieces. One for you, one for me. I'm bringing them out when I've changed my clothes.

              (DAVID exits.)

JENNIFER: Listen. The children are calling again.

              How lovely the trees. In this light. The branches dip, the leaves quiver, they flash the light. Like Morse code, is it? Do they do Morse code with light?

              We have no children. We have good jobs. But no security. We're saving the limit every year in RRSPs.

              (DAVID comes out.)

              David? I want him to stay a while, to come to visit me sometimes. I can talk to him. I can say things I want to say. I can talk the way I want to talk.

DAVID: Yes well, that's because he's mute, isn't it? He's mute or he's pretending to be mute for his own purposes. Maybe he's deaf too. Eh? *(To BOB.)* Are you deaf? Deaf and dumb?

JENNIFER: David.

DAVID: Christ.

JENNIFER: He's not deaf. He listens. He listens when people talk.

DAVID: You're a good pair then aren't you?

JENNIFER: I hate the way we talk. Snippets. That's the way we talk. In snippets of sarcasm.

        (DAVID goes inside.)

        Do you remember last night I was talking about bones? You make me think. Someday maybe people will find our bones, hundreds of thousands of years from now. They'll wonder how we lived.

        (JENNIFER goes inside. BOB constructs a makeshift, childish tent with a blanket and crawls into it.

        Morning. Very bright. BOB is sleeping on the deck in the tent. DAVID comes with his briefcase and stands looking at the tent.)

DAVID: Jennifer!

        (JENNIFER comes out.)

        I guess I didn't make myself clear last night. I want him gone. That direct enough for you? It's not what you want to hear. I know that. It's what I want. Let's say, just for the sake of argument, that half the time you get what you want and half the time I get what I want. You've had yours. I want him gone. And you'd better do it quick or you'll be late for work.

        (DAVID goes to his office. JENNIFER can hear him but would rather not. BOB takes his blanket and follows his hand off.

        DAVID's office. He's talking on the dictaphone. His briefcase is nearby, closed.)

July 16th. Personal memorandum. Not for dictation. Message to my wife: Jennifer.

Things have not been good here at the office. I haven't wanted to disturb you—

Maybe it's only a temporary problem.

> *(Early evening. A soft green light.*
>
> *DAVID comes home from work.)*

Jennifer?

JENNIFER: Hi.

DAVID: Hi.

JENNIFER: You know, when I close my eyes tonight, I'm going to see weeds. I pulled weeds all day. And there's still more of them.

DAVID: Marjorie called the office. I told her you were sick.

JENNIFER: Good.

DAVID: I told her you'd be going to the doctor tomorrow if you're still sick. And you'll call her.

JENNIFER: Okay. God, look at my hands.

DAVID: You want to go out for dinner?

JENNIFER: I made a stew. Out of the rest of the leftover steak.

DAVID: Okay.

> *(DAVID walks into house.)*

> *(Off.)* Smells great.

JENNIFER: I kind of like cooking. Sometimes.

> *(JENNIFER walks into house. The following is all offstage.)*

DAVID: Is there any wine left?

JENNIFER: Yes. Should I open a bottle?

DAVID: Sure.

(Sound of music, romantic saxophone.)

JENNIFER: Oh—that's nice.

(He has come to her.)

You're nice.

DAVID: Am I?

(They are kissing.)

You are too. Nice to come home to.

(The music fades out. The GIRL wanders into the yard. It's night, it's windy, the trees are restless. She seems lost, and wanders off.

Another evening. A leftover restlessness in the air.

JENNIFER is sitting on the deck, very dressed up, with quite a lot of jewellery and make-up. She sees DAVID in the distance. She turns and BOB appears with his blanket and follows his hand to her.

DAVID approaches them.)

DAVID: What is this? Jennifer? Are you going somewhere?

JENNIFER: No.

DAVID: Why are you dressed like this?

JENNIFER: I just felt like it.

DAVID: Why is that?

JENNIFER: I don't know.

DAVID: You went to work today, didn't you?

JENNIFER: No. I decided I'm going to quit.

DAVID: Don't be silly.

JENNIFER: It's not silly. I've thought it through.

DAVID: You can't afford to quit.

(DAVID takes BOB by the arm and marches him off. He returns alone. JENNIFER goes and gets BOB and leads him back. DAVID takes his arm again.)

JENNIFER: Leave Bob alone.

DAVID: Bob?

JENNIFER: I decided to call him Bob. I have to call him something. If I find out his real name, I'll call him that.

DAVID: Bob, be a pal. Take a hike.

JENNIFER: David, let's say for the sake of argument that you get what you want half the time and I get what I want half the time. This is what I want. Today. He'll stay out here on the deck.

DAVID: You're nuts.

JENNIFER: He doesn't even like coming into the house. He likes sleeping outside.

DAVID: And where does he like going to the bathroom?

JENNIFER: He uses the bathroom in the house.

DAVID: Fuck. I don't need this, Jennifer. *(To BOB.)* Hey. You—

JENNIFER: Bob.

DAVID: Look. Call him Bob. Call him Dick. Get him the fuck away from my house.

(DAVID goes off to his office. JENNIFER and BOB remain on the deck. Before DAVID speaks, JENNIFER applies more make-up and adds some

jewellery. She enjoys choosing the jewellery, as a child would, playing dress-up. But then she hears DAVID and feels sad for him.)

July...something.

Personal memorandum not for dictation, message for my wife: Dear Jennifer: Things aren't getting any better at work.

I don't think it's a problem that's going to go away.

(BOB jumps up and leaves. DAVID returns.)

DAVID: So, where is he?

JENNIFER: Well it's your night David.

DAVID: It's my night?

JENNIFER: It's your night to have what you want. Which is no Bob.

DAVID: *(Stroking her cheek.)* What's all this? You don't normally wear all this make-up. Or all this jewellery.

JENNIFER: I just feel like it.

DAVID: It's a bit much. Jennifer, I need to talk to you about work. Things aren't going so well.

JENNIFER: Quit.

DAVID: You didn't quit? Did you?

JENNIFER: Yes.

              I don't like the way we live.

              What's wrong?

DAVID: Everything.

JENNIFER: At least we agree.

DAVID: Maybe we need to get away. A couple of days. I could take off at noon tomorrow—a long week-end—

JENNIFER:　　Bob's coming tomorrow.

DAVID:　　I really want some time with you.

> (DAVID goes to his office. JENNIFER adds more make-up and jewellery. DAVID, into his recorder:)

I fear someone is plotting my downfall. Someone wants my job.

My plan is... I have no plan.

We need to get away.

> (DAVID and JENNIFER meet and walk to an out-door café. They sit at a table. DAVID has his brief-case. There is a carafe of wine. The WAITER, played by JOHN, stands over them. He is one of those waiters who wants you to know he's in charge.)

WAITER:　　Our menu sir.

DAVID:　　I'll have the special.

WAITER:　　Our menu madam.

JENNIFER:　　*(To DAVID.)* What is it?

DAVID:　　Salmon.

JENNIFER:　　I'll have that. Wait. Is it poached?

WAITER:　　It's grilled with butter and rosemary.

JENNIFER:　　Oh well, I'll still have it.

> (The WAITER exits. JENNIFER raises her glass.)

It's good to get away.

Lovely to sit under trees.

DAVID:　　*(Thinking he's seen BOB.)* Christ.

JENNIFER: What?

DAVID: If that guy's here—

JENNIFER: What?

DAVID: Bob. If he's here—

JENNIFER: —He isn't here.

DAVID: If you told him—

JENNIFER: I didn't. I didn't say where we were going.

DAVID: Okay. It probably wasn't him. Fuck, the guy's got me psyched out. Think I'm seeing him a hundred miles from home.

(BOB appears, passing behind DAVID so only JENNIFER can see him. She is shocked.)

You know Jennifer, we need to talk.

JENNIFER: David... David, I'm sorry, I don't know what to do.

(The WAITER arrives with two plates. BOB lurches across his path. JENNIFER and DAVID watch, helpless, as the WAITER and BOB collide. The WAITER drops the plates.)

WAITER: Watch where you're going, for Christ's sake.

(BOB staggers off. DAVID and JENNIFER stand. DAVID exits. The WAITER exits. BOB returns, drinks from one of the glasses and picks up a piece of salmon from the ground. He sits at the table like a member of royalty and eats. The WAITER walks out.)

What the fuck— What the fuck do you think you're doing? That's enough of that.

(The WAITER advances menacingly and BOB jumps up and leaves. The WAITER exits. JENNIFER gets BOB and brings him home.)

JENNIFER: You see, don't you? It's become impossible. I know I seem to be saying one thing and wanting another but...David needs me.

> (BOB *slowly assumes a fetal position. She doesn't notice.*)

Bob, you do see?

Do you hear the children? In the summer, children own the world.

> (*She sees him.*)

Bob?

> (*She gathers him to her. He snuggles in like a baby. She undoes her blouse and offers him a breast. His right hand idly strokes her hair. They are, both of them, blissful.*)

(*Sings.*) "Lullaby, and goodnight. With angels delight—"

> (*DAVID enters and stands watching them. DAVID opens his case.*)

It's empty.

DAVID: They haven't been giving me any work.

JENNIFER: But you bring work home. All the time.

DAVID: I bring this home. To make me look good. To people who don't know they aren't giving me any work. They're still paying me. That won't last much longer. They're waiting for me to do the honourable thing, and quit.

JENNIFER: If the world was going to end today, none of this would matter.

DAVID: It matters precisely because the world isn't going to end.

(JENNIFER watches as DAVID goes to sit on the park bench. He opens his briefcase. There are balls inside. He strokes them and raises one to rub against his cheek.)

JENNIFER: You see don't you? David? You see he needs me. He isn't a baby. Of course he isn't. But he needs me like a baby. He needs to be babied. To be mothered. You know, maybe it's a patterning thing. I think they call it patterning. Ducklings follow their mothers. That's how they learn. I think he must have lacked patterning. But if we start over, like this, start with him as a baby, then I think I can raise him. Yes, raise him. Take him through the stages.

DAVID: You think he didn't go through stages?

JENNIFER: Not with love.

DAVID: Are you sure you're thinking of his needs?

JENNIFER: He seems to need this. If I need it too, it's a perfect fit, isn't it?

DAVID: Oh perfect. How long do you expect it to take? And how do you expect to finance it?

JENNIFER: That's just like you.

DAVID: Sorry. You're right.

(JENNIFER watches as DAVID opens his briefcase and sticks his head inside. JENNIFER starts playing on a blanket on the floor with BOB. She is trying to help him sit up. When he rolls over they both laugh and try again. They thoroughly enjoy one another.

Doorbell. JENNIFER answers. ANNE stands in the doorway to talk to her. ANNE is wearing odd make-up and clothes. She looks like MARIE but also like JENNIFER.)

JENNIFER: Oh hello Anne.

ANNE: Jennifer, could I come in?

                (*Long pause while ANNE stares at BOB.*)

                I came to ask advice. I'm worried about John.

JENNIFER: The last I heard John was doing fine. The last I heard he'd been given David's office and David's job.

ANNE: Yes. Is David here?

JENNIFER: No.

ANNE: Is John here?

JENNIFER: Why would John be here?

ANNE: I don't know where he is. He hasn't been home. He hasn't been to work. I thought he was angry with me but it seems it's more serious.

JENNIFER: Why would he be angry with you?

ANNE: I'm afraid I criticized him.

JENNIFER: Goodness. Where would we all be if everyone criticized everyone else? What was the matter?

ANNE: He's started speaking with a German accent. It's silly of course. But he won't stop. He goes on and on speaking with this phony German accent—he doesn't even do it well. Why German, I asked him. God, they lost two world wars.

JENNIFER: Anne, what do you want me to do?

ANNE: I don't know. We worked so hard for this and he's throwing it all away.

JENNIFER: Worked so hard for this…?

ANNE: For his promotion.

JENNIFER: For him to take over David's job.

ANNE: That's coincidental.

JENNIFER: I don't think I have any advice.

ANNE: I must say your own life seems to have taken an
             odd turn.   .

JENNIFER: Yes. It was nice of you to drop by Anne. Good to
             see you again.

             (JENNIFER shepherds ANNE out the door.)

             (To herself.) How good of you to come. *(To BOB.)*
             Where were we Pooh Bear? Oh yes we were teach-
             ing you to sit up all by your own-self, weren't we?
             Come on my Bobsy-Wobsy, that's a boy. Show
             Mummy what a big boy you are. Up with his arms!
             He's a big boy!

             *(They laugh hard, BOB silently. JENNIFER still
             watches DAVID who remains on the bench, bob-
             bing his head into his case. JOHN enters.)*

JOHN: Yah vell, you see Jennifer, all zat I say iss falsse. Or
             at least now I don't know ze difference. I am so
             ussed to speaking falsse I vouldn't know if I vas
             speaking true. Zis vay, you know, people, zey are
             varned.

             Anne, she can't understand. Vy German? she asks.
             Zey are losers. Zey lost two vorld vars for Gott's
             sake. Vy German? I don't know. I saw a lot of var
             movies ven I vass a kid. Ze Germans in ze movies
             ver shifty, dishonest and mean. Vat can I say? She
             vouldn't understand me vatever I say. Vatever I
             say iss not for sending messages from me to her,
             it's only for pushing me up the ladder of success,
             it's only for plans und schemes. I've done vith
             plans und schemes. I took David's job. Zat vass my
             last planning und scheming.

JENNIFER: I think Anne cares about you.

JOHN: Yah, she cares I'm not smart enough to fake Japa-
                   nese. Look how zey get ahead in ze vorld.

                   Ah maybe once she cared about me. I vass falsse
                   vith her too. Vomen. It vasn't good. Lots of time I
                   left her lonely.

                   I vass thinking maybe I could move in vith you. Vat
                   vith David gone. I can't go back to vork now. Zey
                   vould laugh me out of ze office now.

                   (He walks authoritatively past JENNIFER.)

                   I know you haff empty rooms in zis big house. I am
                   certain zere iss a room for me. Ya, ya.

                   (He exits. ANNE enters, looking more eccentric.)

ANNE: I know he's here. I saw him come in here. Don't lie
                   Jennifer. It's not nice.

JENNIFER: He is here. He doesn't want to see you.

ANNE: He doesn't want to. He doesn't want to. Why is he
                   here? Is he still speaking with that stupid German
                   accent? Look, can't you make him stop? Just make
                   him stop? Just make him stop? Just make him stop?
                   Just make him stop? Just—

                   (She blanks out, freezes like a statue.)

JENNIFER: Anne? Anne?

                   (JENNIFER tries to move her, wake her.)

                   John? John, you have to come here. Please?

                   *(JENNIFER gets JOHN and shows him ANNE.
                   JOHN makes ANNE sit. She sits like a statue, im-
                   mobile and uninvolved. JOHN stands by like a sol-
                   dier.*

                   *JENNIFER begins spoon-feeding BOB. BOB keeps
                   spitting food out. She keeps trying. He spits it in her
                   face. She slaps him. He cries hard, soundlessly.*

The blackboard appears. "Our Theory of Goodness"
is written on it. JENNIFER starts shaking badly,
once in a while shuddering violently.)

JOHN: "Our Seeory of Gootness". Ya? You see, Annie, my
         love? I vill instruct you. Annie my love. Raise your
         arm for gootness sake, Anne.

         (He lifts her arm into a Nazi salute.)

         You learn ze lesson, ya? You're a good girl now. Ya,
         ya, at your best now.

JENNIFER: Where's David?

         I want David.

JOHN: Do you sink he'd come home to zis brat? Zis brat iss
         the reason he left.

JENNIFER: You're the reason he left.

JOHN: No no. I ousted him from hiss job. I admit zat. I had
         nossing to do vith hiss leaving home. Get rid of ze
         brat und he'll come home.

         (BOB toddles over and knocks over the easel.)

         Brat!

JENNIFER: Bobby, come here.

         (But BOB marches around, following his hand.)

JOHN: Aw don't feel bad. Zere arc consolations, eh? Here
         ve are, you got a brat und no husband, I got a vife,
         she's a zombie. What could be more natural zan
         you und me...? It's vat you vant, you know. It's not
         a child you vant. You vant a man.

         (BOB grabs a knife and offers it to JENNIFER.)

         Hey. Hey now. That's enough of that.

         (JOHN hides behind ANNE. JENNIFER puts the
         knife away. She gathers BOB to her, rocks him.)

Needs a good whipping, ze brat.

(They freeze.

BOB pulls away and goes to the park bench. The others remain frozen, JENNIFER with her arms out. BOB follows his hand to DAVID and sits beside him. He curls up on the bench. DAVID pats BOB's head. BOB rises and leads DAVID home. They join the tableau. JENNIFER removes her clothes and jewellery to reveal a simple white dress.

Happy music plays: Menuhin and Grappelli, "Jealousy". A festive, speckled light.

All shift to the back yard, under the tree. The table from the dream in Part One reappears, laden with food set in coloured jellies. DAVID is ensconced in the seat of honour. JOHN remains as stiff as a soldier. ANNE remains in a trance, seated on the park bench, which is now part of the backyard. They all sit eating, pretending nothing is wrong. JOHN is once in a while force-feeding ANNE.)

JOHN: I hat to ask you all to forgiff me.

DAVID: I had to forgive you all.

JENNIFER: Now we are having a feast. To celebrate we're having a feast. David is home. All is forgiven.

(BOB begins happily banging his spoon to the music. DAVID picks up his spoon and joins him, then JOHN starts. At the same time, they are gobbling their food and drink, groaning their appreciation, tossing bones and scraps over their shoulders. The men push food into ANNE's mouth with their fingers. And pour wine into her. They may "talk" to each other in sentences that have rhythm but no words or meaning.

JENNIFER becomes subdued, watching JOHN. JOHN grabs JENNIFER and molests her, in their sight. DAVID hides his head in his briefcase. BOB grabs the knife and waves it at JENNIFER. He insists she take the knife. The three of them struggle and she kills JOHN.

BOB marches up and down, triumphant, then stops.

JENNIFER goes to ANNE, who remains immobile. She cuddles into ANNE's arms. A wedge-shaped shadow gradually falls over them, fitting the shape they make. ANNE shifts into a new, painfully contorted position. JENNIFER separates from her, then imitates her.

The GIRL walks on, carrying "A Girl of the Limberlost". Seeing her, JENNIFER comes out of her pose and makes room for her on the bench. The GIRL opens the book and with deep satisfaction reads:)

GIRL: "To all girls of the Limberlost
                             in general
                             and one
                      Jennifer Ellen Martin
                         in particular."

(She hugs the book to her.

The End.)